Original title:
Finding Purpose Between the Pages

Copyright © 2025 Creative Arts Management OÜ
All rights reserved.

Author: Dorian Ashford
ISBN HARDBACK: 978-1-80566-171-9
ISBN PAPERBACK: 978-1-80566-466-6

Between Covers

In a book, I took a peek,
Hoping for wisdom, or just a tweak.
But I found a cat, curled up tight,
Purposely napping, what a sight!

Pages flipped, tea spilled in glee,
Where's the moral? Can't you see?
Just a tale of socks gone wrong,
Yet I laughed; it felt so strong!

A Life Revealed

Turned the page, a life displayed,
Beau from the office, unafraid.
In spandex shorts, he danced so grand,
Now that's a story, oh, how bland!

Life is wild, a comedic trip,
Like a hula hoop that won't grip.
But in the book of highs and lows,
I found my flair in a dance that flows!

The Richness of Written Silence

In silence, words soft as a cloud,
Twinkling quietly, oh so proud.
Like a librarian shushing a sneeze,
Irony dances, if you please!

Their whispers are giggles, silent screams,
Pages brushing past in dreams.
Each chapter a snack of thoughts gone wild,
Could this be chaos beautifully compiled?

Tales of Transformation

A frog in a book thought he'd roam,
Then found himself far from home.
From polka dots to a crown of gold,
Kissed by a prince? That's just bold!

Transformation leads to a laugh,
Who knew reading could spark this craft?
Frog to king? Oh, what a twist,
But that saga? I might've missed!

The Palette of Poetic Purpose

A poet with colors, oh so free,
Dipped a brush in upturned tea.
Painting a scene with rhymes so bright,
But why is that cat still in sight?

Roses are red, the sky is blue,
Yet cats make better artwork too!
In every stanza, a chuckle's grace,
Life's a canvas; we're all out of place!

Sifting Through Stories

In a world of books and tales,
I stumbled on stories that never fail.
Dancing words with funny quirks,
A dragon who cooks, and one that jerks.

The romance flew, then slipped and flopped,
Pages turning, and I just stopped.
Amidst the laughter, a lesson peeked,
My purpose shouted, though it creaked.

The Alchemy of Written Thought

Mixing potions, ink and rhyme,
A wizard's pen, way ahead of time.
Concocting plots with a dash of sass,
Who knew the hero could trip over grass?

In my mind, castles take flight,
Yet my fingers fumble, oh what a sight!
Tales of wisdom wrapped in jest,
With every page, I'm on a quest.

Syllables of Self-Discovery

A syllable here, a giggle there,
Words collide in the air, oh beware!
Tripping through lines of misplaced dreams,
I found my purpose amid the meme streams.

Characters, quirky, come alive,
An astronaut trying to learn to drive.
With every chapter, I lost my way,
But laughter echoed, come what may.

The Library of Lost Aspirations

In a shelf stacked high with faded hopes,
I met a philosopher who juggled ropes.
He said, 'Dream big, but don't hit the wall!'
As he tripped over books, I had a ball.

Pages flutter like confused birds,
Holding secrets, laughs, and quirky words.
Through dust and laughter, I took a look,
In this library, it's all a hook!

The Book of Life's Questions

Why does the hero always win?
Is pudding a dessert or a sin?
Do cats have secret meetings at night?
And is chocolate really a superfood bite?

In quests for wisdom, we often seek,
Through tales of dragons and a talking beak.
If all books could talk, oh what they'd say,
I'd bet they'd complain about wear and fray.

Every turn of the page holds a jest,
Even Shakespeare's ghosts have a silly quest.
What if the truth lies in a comic strip?
Life's puzzles solved with a sarcastic quip!

So grab that novel, don't be shy,
Dive into absurdity, oh my, oh my!
Between the lines, humor will dance,
Let's twist those fables, take a chance!

Whispers from the Spine

In the old library, secrets abound,
Books confide, though no one's around.
A dusty tome might just have the scoop,
On why socks disappear in the laundry loop!

Each spine must tremble, for wit is near,
Droll dramas unfold, bring on the cheer!
Is that a plot twist or just my tea?
I swear the shelves winked at me, do you see?

When pages flip, giggles grow loud,
As characters scheme, they make me proud.
Perhaps a romance with a quirky duck,
Or a villain whose plans misfire? How luck!

So listen closely when you're alone,
Books spill the beans in their own funny tone.
Between the whispers, find quirky delight,
In every word, let laughter take flight!

Epiphanies Encased in Print

Turn the page, await the surprise,
A cat wearing glasses? Oh how it ties!
Wisdom wears sneakers; it's quite absurd,
But that's how you'll swallow the funniest word.

The punchline's hidden in metaphors deep,
Writing it down makes sure it won't leap.
Like life's riddle wrapped nicely in prose,
Or a pun so bad, it surely unloads.

Every book claims it's got the best scoop,
Yet some are so weird they make one droop.
Just understand this one vital thing:
Laughter is found in the silliest fling!

So read on, reader, and laugh with glee,
In the margins, quirky notes could be.
Profound truths wrapped in silliness fit,
Life's nibs of wisdom, beyond every wit!

Lighthouses in the Library

Navigating shelves like a ship at sea,
Each cover a lighthouse shining for me.
The beacon of humor, it guides the way,
Through nautical nonsense, I laugh and sway.

Lost in the stories, I catch a big wave,
Pirates chase rabbits, oh how they behave!
Exotic adventures with a comedic spin,
Where jokes are treasures, let the fun begin!

As I sail through, maps of mindless fun,
Crumbling clichés caught in the run.
Plot holes like whirlpools, oh what a mess,
But smoother the journey, I must confess!

So raise the sails, let the humor combine,
In every corner, wisdom does entwine.
Each book a lighthouse, guiding my muse,
In this vast library, I shall never lose!

The Journey Through Ink

In a bookshop, I found my fate,
Among the books, I had to wait.
The dust bunnies danced in a row,
I laughed as they put on a show.

My coffee cup spilled a tale untold,
As I searched for stories, oh so bold.
Between chapters, I tripped on a plot,
Who knew my life tied to a knot?

The author scribbled with flair,
While I battled paper cuts and despair.
Each page turned was a jolly tease,
With side notes of humor and wheezy wheeze.

In the margins, I wrote my dreams,
With ink splotches like silly memes.
The journey is wacky, but who's to say?
I'll keep reading, come what may!

Beneath the Surface of Prose

In the depths of a novel, I found a fish,
It flopped and floundered, granting my wish.
Beneath the surface, it made a scene,
With bubbles of laughter, like a comedy queen.

Each chapter swam with unexpected twists,
Like pirates in tights with a treasure of lists.
The words giggled loudly from page to page,
As I entered the bookworm stage.

I took a dip in the well of puns,
Where metaphors swam and cracked up for fun.
I surfaced with giggles and ink-stained hands,
In a world where humor makes all the plans.

So let's dive deeper, let's take a leap,
Into the pools of prose where the funny fish creep.
With laughter and joy, I'll float along,
In the currents of stories, I'll find where I belong!

The Light of Unturned Leaves

In a bookstore's corner, I found a gem,
With pages aglow, a delightful diadem.
The leaves turned lightly, like fluttering wings,
With secrets hidden and silly things.

I flipped to a chapter with muffins galore,
And a cat on a mission to settle a score.
The light of the words made my heart sing,
As characters plotted their amusing king.

Oh, the snacks they shared, with a wink and a grin,
Made me ponder the meaning of undercooked sin.
Each bite was a giggle, a mirthful surprise,
In this world where the ordinary dies.

I basked in the glow of a comical plight,
While chapters unfolded in pure sheer delight.
So let's savor the laughter, let's dance on the leaves,
For every page turned, a new joy it weaves!

Mapping the Uncharted Lines

With a compass of words, I set out to roam,
In the land of plots, I made my home.
Each line was a joke, each map had a laugh,
Like a knight in a parallel universe of craft.

I charted the territories of whimsical plots,
Where walrus philosophers gave me their thoughts.
With every direction, a chuckle arose,
In an atlas adorned with poetic prose.

I sketched out my journey with crayons of glee,
As squirrels debated the meaning of tea.
The margins held secrets and doodles so bright,
That tickled my fancy, oh what a sight!

So let's take the plunge into literary maps,
Where humor and wisdom collide with mishaps.
I'll follow the ink trails, come laugh with me,
In this land of adventure, so wild and free!

The Story Beneath the Surface

In a tome where socks go to hide,
Adventurers stumble, jaws open wide.
The cat chapters lace up for a dance,
While the footnotes plot their mischief and prance.

A wizard's spell to find lost keys,
Casts a laugh as they munch on peas.
With each turn, a giggle spills,
As dragons chase their own tail thrills.

Scribes of the Soul

Quills dipped in jello, ink made of dreams,
Scribes scribble nonsense, bursting at seams.
A penguin writes sonnets, a verse for the chill,
While the goldfish debates if it's time to grill.

Every page flip is a dance of surprise,
A banana peel fumbles, oh how it flies!
Characters tumble, writing's a spree,
Laughs echo wild, as raucous as can be.

Verses of the Unseen Voyage

On ships made of pizza, we sail through the crust,
With toppings of laughter, adventure is a must.
As anchovies whisper of deep-sea delight,
We voyage through laughter, not a serious sight.

The wind's a zephyr of tickles and cheer,
Sailing past dragons that hiccup from beer.
Unseen journeys compel us to roam,
Each verse wraps us in joy—we're home!

The Odyssey of Each Word

Words waddle about in a nonsensical race,
With rhyme schemes that twist, what a silly place!
Vowels cavort while consonants play,
In a party of phrases, they wiggle away.

An apostrophe winks, a comma takes flight,
While verbs throw a bash that lasts through the night.
In this odyssey strange, we giggle and learn,
Every misstep turns into a turn!

Ink Trails and Shadows

In a bookshop lost, I stroll,
Chasing stories, just for the soul.
A cat on a shelf gives me a glare,
Like my jokes—too much to bear.

The novels whisper, 'Pick me up!',
While coffee spills like a clumsy cup.
I trip on a tale, what a disgrace,
Can laughter be found in this wild chase?

Between the chapters, I take a peek,
Are these real lives, or just a leak?
Characters dance, so full of flair,
While I search for where I fit in here.

With paper cuts like battle scars,
I turn the pages, wish on stars.
In pages filled with dreams and schemes,
Who knew wisdom comes with caffeine themes?

A Canvas of Thoughts

With crayons and ink, I scribble away,
My art resembles a terrible play.
A masterpiece hits the room, and I cringe,
With colors so bright, they make you cringe.

Each stroke is a laugh, a wild, silly fate,
My canvas screams, 'You should wait!'
Yet here I am, splattering dreams,
Hoping one day, I'll have bursts of beams.

Puzzles of chaos, ink spills and smears,
With laughter erupting, dissolving my fears.
I can't draw a straight line to save my life,
But hey, it's not bad—unless there's strife!

The colors fumble, as I join the fray,
In my own mixed-up, artistic ballet.
I paint with intent, or so I say,
In hopes to discover my bright, funny way.

Tracing Footprints of Wisdom

Walking on wisdom, shoes made of jokes,
Every footstep lands with giggles and pokes.
In a crowd of thinkers, I fumble and slip,
Cringing at every smart-aleck quip.

Footprints abound, on paths of the mind,
Where wisdom and laughter are more closely aligned.
I trip on the logic, it sounds so absurd,
Like trying to fly with a very slow bird.

Searching for answers while laughing out loud,
The search for that wisdom just draws quite a crowd.
Should I take notes, or simply just grin?
Too much to ponder—where does one begin?

But in the end, should that wisdom be found,
I'll wear it like shoes, round and quite bound.
For life's silly journey of learning to cope,
Is best when it's filled with now-unicorn hope.

Tales Carved in Silence

In a library quiet, the stories all hum,
Yet here I am, tapping the drum.
The silence thickens, an odd kind of breeze,
Like waiting for someone to sneeze.

On shelves stacked high with tales galore,
I search for a one that might make me roar.
But every time I reach, I find only dust,
Like all my resolutions—they're filled with rust.

Characters form but can't find their pitch,
I chuckle at them like I'm at a glitch.
Their stories unfold, but I can't keep track,
Do they laugh or cry? When will I crack?

With whispers of wisdom in the library hush,
I laugh in the dark, my thoughts all a rush.
So here I sit, with a grin and a book,
Hoping for laughter—not that grave look.

The Tapestry of Tales

In a bookshop corner, I chanced to reside,
Amidst tales of dragons and mythical pride.
I tried to locate all my lost socks,
But ended up tangled in storybook blocks.

A wise old penguin gave me advice,
He said, "Read my tales; they're cozy and nice."
So I flipped through pages with great delight,
And laughed at the plots that took flight at night.

The characters danced in a whimsical play,
While I searched for wisdom in a quirky way.
I found a banana and a frog on the run,
And thought, "This is better than being outdone!"

So now with my snacks and my favorite tome,
I trust that the tales will lead me back home.
Each book I encounter, each plot that I trace,
Adds a swirl to the fabric of this funny space.

Inkblots and Dreams

With inkblots aplenty and dreams to ignite,
I scribbled my thoughts long into the night.
Pages would giggle, they held secrets deep,
While I searched for clarity in Adam's sleep.

A purple giraffe whispered, "Give it a try,
To pen all your hopes and watch them fly high!"
I wrote about donuts and dancing floors,
Each ink splatter opened up hidden doors.

Yet socks keep disappearing beneath all the fluff,
My cat finds them first – I can't get enough!
But amidst the confusion, I laughed with glee,
As I swirled through the pages, a whimsical spree.

So here in my chaos, joyfully I glean,
The purpose within is not always seen.
Each line I embrace, with a chuckle, a beam,
Brings me closer to treasures within every dream.

In Pursuit of Literary Light

With a cap tilted sideways and a pen on the go,
I scoured the shelves for a character's glow.
Where could they be hiding, those beings so grand?
Under piles of novels, they staged a stand!

A cactus in verse whispered tales from the past,
And urged me to ponder, "Will hilarity last?"
So I typed on my keyboard, a dance with the muse,
Unraveling laughter, it's all mine to use.

In the margins, I found a bewildered hare,
Who shouted, "Write faster! Your snacks are laid bare!"
His antics encouraged a story so light,
Filled with giggles and nonsense, a comical flight.

Through the chapters of life and the stories I weave,
I discovered there's magic, if you just believe.
Each quirk and each chuckle, a treasure in sight,
Brings laughter to pages, like shimmering light.

Reveries between the Lines

A coffee cup's dance on a table so round,
Whispers of nonsense in margins I found.
In reveries formed between sips and sighs,
The plots took on mischief, much to my surprise.

A cat in a hat and a toaster that sings,
Spoke volumes of laughter, of silly old things.
Each character spun tales with delightful grins,
All wrapped in the joy where the weirdness begins.

In the forest of fiction, under trees made of prose,
I ambled with giggles and tickles on toes.
Found a squirrel with stories that tickled my soul,
And a penguin that juggled, pretty out of control!

So here in the margins, my dreams come alive,
With absurdity swirling, I cheerfully thrive.
Each line I concoct, a laughter-filled dance,
And revel in stories, not leaving to chance!

A Quest for Clarity Within

I searched through books both old and new,
For wisdom hiding, what to do?
I found a guide that led me here,
A coffee mug, to hold my cheer.

A chapter lost, a verse gone rogue,
I flipped the pages, cursed the fog.
With every line, I laughed aloud,
At plots so wild, they drew a crowd.

Plot twists sharp like knives of jest,
Characters forgot their own quest.
With every read, I swayed and swirled,
In this bizarre literary world.

So here I sit, my book in hand,
Digesting tales both grand and bland.
In this mad quest, I've found my muse,
A whimsical ride through the author's views.

The Written Compass

In dusty tomes and stories bold,
I sought direction, truth untold.
A map was drawn, or so I thought,
But all I got was tangled plot.

With every turn, the ink did dance,
Characters pranced in comical chance.
I lost my way in whimsical lines,
Chasing shadows; oh how it shines!

A compass made of paper clips,
Guided me through literary flips.
Each sentence led me round and round,
In laughter's grip, I was tightly bound.

At last, I laughed and closed the tome,
A detour's fun; I'm still at home.
With metaphorical directions so bright,
I'll wander forever in delight!

Light in Literary Loopholes

In every plot, there lurks a catch,
Creative loopholes feed the batch.
I slipped through pages, fell in glee,
As characters bumbled right past me.

A twist in dialogue, a laugh to share,
Every author's sneaky little dare.
They wrote the rules, then lost the key,
Unlocking joy, what a sight to see!

When story lines began to stray,
I cheered them on, hip-hip-hooray!
Each chapter's dance a jolly spree,
With words that tickle, so delightfully free.

So here I roam, through quirks and bends,
In laughter's glow where joy transcends.
A journey wrapped in silly prose,
In literary loopholes, fun just grows!

Reflections in the Reflection

I gazed upon the mirror's glare,
A character's face began to stare.
In words I saw a wink and grin,
Who knew reflections could be this thin?

Each line I read, the more I laughed,
In anecdotes, they shared their craft.
A pun here, a jest right there,
My bookish buddy beyond compare.

With every glance, absurdities peak,
As stories chime in eccentric speak.
Reflections blur, but spirits rise,
In this quirky world, we harmonize!

So here's to mirth in every verse,
A merry chase through humor's purse.
In pages deep, let laughter sail,
As I embrace this fanciful trail.

Fragments of Self Amongst the Text

In the margins, doodles thrive,
Drawn by kids who feel alive.
Between the lines, I seek my fate,
But mostly just check for lunch break.

A plot twist here, a pun there,
Characters act without a care.
Lost in tales both wild and grand,
I swear my plot's got out-of-hand!

The mystery spills, the humor flows,
In every chapter, laughter grows.
Finding lessons in each joke,
Who knew a novel hid so much hope?

With every flip, a giggle bursts,
As I chase after my own thirst.
Through silly tales and wacky lines,
This bookish life's full of sweet signs.

The Silent Oath of the Reader

I swear to read with snacks in hand,
Bread crumbs fall, they litter the land.
With chocolate bars and chips galore,
Each page turn leads to crumbs on the floor.

The hero stumbles, I chime in cheer,
Right when the villain's drawing near.
I laugh at mishaps, I roll my eyes,
These paper tales are quite the surprise!

Every chapter a new delight,
I share my thoughts, though they're out of sight.
For every twist that makes me grin,
I mark the moment and dive right in.

And if the ending's rather lame,
I'll improvise, give it a new name.
Pages whisper, they weave and twine,
In my own mind, the stars align!

Chronicles of the Heart

In the epic tales where dreams collide,
I flip through pages, my trusty guide.
With heroes bold and villains sly,
I often laugh, I seldom cry.

Plot holes beckon, like sirens' calls,
Except my heart's still on the walls.
From fantasy lands to the mundane,
I dance through stories, like a comet's train.

With hiccuped joys and rhymes so odd,
Each character feels like a very good fraud.
The laughter echoes, the fun extends,
In my fiction realm, the joy never ends!

So here's to the stories, wild and free,
Where every twist is a cup of tea.
Crack a smile, turn the page anew,
And let the magic connect me and you!

Threads of Meaning in the Fabric of Words

With every thread, a story spins,
A fabric woven where mischief begins.
Some tales are bright, while others are frayed,
But in laughter's seam, all fears are swayed.

Plot-twists tug at the seams of fate,
Characters dance on their own plate.
My morning coffee spills, story rants,
While I ponder why my socks wear pants!

Every line a thread, a quirk, a twist,
Missed connections, lost in the mist.
An epic novel that leads to a fall,
Where even the bookmark has its own call!

Let's stitch together tales so absurd,
In this grand tapestry, nothing's deterred.
For in every chapter, humor resides,
A furry monster just wants to ride!

Echoes in Margins

In the margins, notes reside,
Where my doodles choose to hide.
A cat in a hat, and a mouse in a tie,
Who knew my journal could make me cry?

Each row of text with a tale untold,
Adventures of socks, and stories of gold.
Twisted plots in squiggled lines,
Is that a plot twist? Or just bad designs?

Coffee stains tell tales of woe,
The plot thickens with every flow.
Characters run from page to page,
Am I the author, or just a sage?

As each chapter slips away,
I ponder the characters' disarray.
Was it humor I sought or grave despair?
Oops! There goes my sandwich in mid-air!

Ink-Stained Revelations

Amid the words, my thoughts take flight,
A penguin on a quest at night.
Seeking truth in a sea of ink,
Where the coffee's strong, and the logic's weak.

The pages grumble, 'This plot is lame!'
A parrot squawks, 'Well, who's to blame?'
I scribble down all the absurd,
A rabbit in a suit? Nah, that's unheard!

As I flip through tales of epic quirks,
A wizard sneezes, and his magic lurks.
Every chapter's a wild ride,
Where even the puns go off asides.

Lost in this world, I trip and tumble,
Finding wisdom in notes that fumble.
If stories teach, then I'm quite the fool,
For all I've learned is just a rule!

Quest Within the Quatrains

Oh, what a quest in four short lines,
With talking squirrels and space-time signs.
The hero trips over his own boots,
While fate delivers strange pursuits!

In a world where plots are rarely flat,
The frog advises, 'Don't trust the cat!'
Adventure waits with every turn,
But hold onto sanity—that I learn!

As I pen my thoughts in the shadiest nook,
I find lost treasure—oh wait, that's a book!
Each verse a riddle, a laugh, a cheer,
Dancing on margins, I know no fear.

With every quatrain and silly scheme,
I chase the moments, I chase the dream.
So join me now on this hilarious ride,
Where searching for meaning is best with pride!

The Lost Manuscript

Once a manuscript, beautifully penned,
Now a saga of gnomes, where squirrels blend.
With every draft, I lose my way,
Did I write a story, or just go play?

In the attic, dust bunnies take a squat,
Watching me scribble, and judging a lot.
I search for coherence in rambling prose,
While the plot escapes, like the cat with my clothes!

Chasing the muse, I trip on my chair,
As the fairy asserts, 'You should really care!'
Yet laughter spills from each crazy line,
In this whirl of chaos, there's humor divine.

So here I stand with pages galore,
Crafting the nonsense I truly adore.
If a guide exists, it's cloaked in fun,
For purpose emerges with each quirky pun!

Pages of Self-Discovery

In a bookshop I did roam,
Searching for my true heart's home.
Each spine whispered stories fresh,
I laughed at my own silly mesh.

With the cookbooks, I did flirt,
About soufflés, I'd act like an expert.
Yet my culinary skills, quite dire,
I just can't seem to boil water on fire.

Mysteries drew me in their clutch,
But my detective skills, not worth much.
Each twist and turn, I took for strife,
Just tripped over my typos in life.

Every page turned felt like a jest,
Plot twists that put my wit to the test.
Each laugh a reminder of what I lack,
But in this funny tale, I'll never look back.

The Parable of Forgotten Pages

In a library dusty and old,
Sat tales of adventure, brave and bold.
I picked one up, heavy as bricks,
Thinking I'd discover eternal tricks.

But the cover said 'read me next year,'
So much for ambitions, let's grab a beer.
Bookmark in hand, I tried to be good,
Then flipped to the end – who knew I'd brood?

Characters running without a care,
While I struggle to comb through my hair.
They had heroes and goblins, all the hype,
I had laundry piling – oh, what a type!

In the end, I laughed at my plight,
These pages taught me to take flight.
For life isn't scripted; it's all just a game,
I'll write my own story, and it won't be the same.

Inked with Intention

With a pen in hand, I start to plot,
A tale of wisdom or maybe not.
I scribble down thoughts, from zany to wise,
Hoping some magic will surface and rise.

My hero is lazy, with snacks piled high,
He leaps over goals with a burger nearby.
In each chapter, he takes a long snooze,
Inspiring me to just lounge in my shoes.

A villain who spills coffee on pages so bright,
Turns best-sellers into a messy sight.
But finding joy in that spilled cup,
Reminds me to laugh and just not give up.

So ink me a tale full of blunders and cheer,
Let each problem dissolve in the beer.
For life's an epic, not meant to be tame,
And as long as I'm laughing, I'm winning the game.

The Chronicles of Longing

In the chapter of want, I flipped through the terms,
Wishing for love, or at least some cute germs.
I jotted down notes of all I adore,
But end up with pizza boxes strewn on the floor.

The hero I crafted, a charming old chap,
But he ended up snoring, oh what a trap!
He searches for romance in a fruit shop aisle,
But all he finds is a melon's sweet smile.

Outside the window, the world goes by fast,
Yet I'm caught in a tale that just won't last.
With whimsical dreams and a heart full of hope,
I wrestle with life, just trying to cope.

So here's to the pages where stories arise,
Filled with laughter, angst, and big surprise.
Each line that I write, a chuckle or two,
That reminds me I'm me, and I'm funny, too!

Seeking Solace in Sentences

In a bookshop nook, I ponder and sigh,
Where the characters plot and the plot bounces high.
I trip on a tome that promises glee,
But it turns out it's just a history spree.

With coffee in hand, I dive into lore,
Hoping to find what I'm really here for.
Pages turn fast, but I'm stuck on a pun,
Is this humor or wisdom? I can't tell—oh, run!

My cat on the shelf, he gives me a glance,
As I wrestle with plots like a twisted romance.
He meows like a critic, quite smug and aloof,
"Please seek your solace; I'm busy, forsooth!"

Yet every adventure brings choices to bear,
In stories, we flounder, like fish in midair.
So I grin at the chaos, and relish the spree,
For between all these pages, there's laughter in me.

The Story Within

Inside every book, there's a tale not so bland,
Each twist and each turn, like a jester's hand.
Characters dance like they're late for a date,
In a plot that's more tangled than my last blind date.

I chuckle at villains who scheme and disguise,
With mustaches and capes, they're quite the surprise.
The hero trips over a banana peel,
And suddenly, all tragedy starts to heal.

Pages are magic, or so they say,
When I'm chasing after words that just won't stay.
A wizard appears with a wink, oh dear,
"Look for your story—and maybe a beer!"

So let's laugh at the lines that twist and turn,
For the humor in every plot is what we earn.
With stories inside and giggles to spin,
The joy of the written is where we begin.

Navigating the Unfolding

Every turn of the page, a riddle in tow,
I navigate madness like I'm in a show.
Characters argue, they shout and they bicker,
I wonder if they know their plot's getting thicker.

On chapters that wobble, I stumble and sway,
Finding punchlines in prose—ah, what a day!
With every surprise, I can't help but grin,
Even when the plot twists turn me within.

The librarian squints, adjusting her specs,
"Dear reader," she says, "keep your cash and your checks!"
But I'm busy discovering jokes in the text,
That charm of the characters—what's coming next?

Here in the margins, I leave little notes,
Sketching funny faces as the adventure floats.
In this saga of letters, I'm lost but just fine,
Because laughing through stories makes all the stars shine.

Echoes of the Written Word

In echoes of pages, I hear laughter loud,
As words dance around like they're part of a crowd.
A plot line of goofballs, a twist or a turn,
Leaves me chuckling, oh, how the tables do churn!

Characters trip over their purposeful fate,
While I sip my tea, they fuss and they debate.
"Why don't you listen?" a sidekick insists,
As dramas unfold with a comedic twist.

So here I am, lost in fictional spree,
With each shared chuckle, I'm light as can be.
From lines that confuse to puns that just ping,
The echoes of stories make my heart sing.

Dear readers unite in this whimsical dream,
Our laughter entwined in a comical theme.
So open your books; let the fun reappear,
For the written word resonates with cheer!

The Rebirth of Words

Once a book sat, gathering dust,
With pages that just seemed to rust.
A reader came, with curious eyes,
And suddenly, those words could fly!

They danced about, they laughed and played,
In every nook, a pun was laid.
From wizards bold to cats that sing,
Oh, how those letters love to swing!

A plot twist here, a laugh right there,
In ink and dreams, we lose our care.
Characters, they simply won't quit,
With each new page, they throw a fit!

So dust them off, those long-lost tomes,
Turn laughter's key to literary homes.
For in each sentence, joy's unfurled,
A rebirth of words that change the world!

Whispers in the Margin

In the margins, secrets dwell,
They giggle softly, cast a spell.
A note from me, a silly quirk,
Is meta-crazy—a total perk!

Oh, look! A doodle, what a sight,
A cat in space, a flying kite.
The words may be serious, yet here,
A tiny smile appears sincere.

As chapters close and open wide,
The scribbles turn into our guide.
Each joke, a map, a merry mark,
Where laughter thrives, igniting spark!

So take a peek, don't be a bore,
In those whispers, there's so much more.
A treasure trove of humor fine,
In every scribble, a chance to shine!

The Ink of Destiny

With ink in hand, I write my fate,
A clumsy scribe, it's never late.
From comical woes to grand escapes,
The plot unfolds with silly shapes!

A hero sneezes—oh, what a plight!
The villain trips, but what a sight!
In every twist, I chuckle loud,
For destiny wears a jester's crown!

The stories flow like spilled milk tea,
I swear that book just laughed at me!
So as I pen, I laugh and cheer,
For ink of destiny isn't drear!

Each sentence sparkles, bright with glee,
In every tale, there's more to see.
A cosmic giggle—it's quite a show,
With every word, we steal the flow!

Unwritten Chapters

In the shelves, a book lies still,
Its pages blank, a paper thrill.
So much potential, oh what a tease,
A chapter waits, for whimsy's breeze!

An open plot, yet nothing planned,
A chance to write with a crazy hand.
What if a llama led the way?
Or aliens danced—a grand ballet!

The unwritten chapters call my name,
With every thought, a spark, a flame.
Should I make monsters bake a pie?
Or have a squirrel reach for the sky?

So here I sit, with giggles bright,
Creating wonders, wielding delight.
In every blank, a laugh untold,
Unwritten chapters—let's be bold!

Reverence for the Written Whisper

In a dusty nook, a book does lay,
Whispering tales of the sloth and the fay.
With coffee stains and a chocolate bar,
Each page reveals just how weird we are.

The hero trips over a cat on the street,
He complains that life's a tricky feat.
But oh, how we laugh at the plot twist,
For every poor choice is just pure bliss.

A wizard in pajamas casts spells in the night,
While goblins swap fables that never sound right.
We giggle at rhymes that don't quite align,
In the realm of the absurd, we sip on our wine.

So let's crack a grin and flip through the tome,
With each turn of a page, find our good home.
Amidst all the laughter, the stories unfold,
With a wink at the writer, as madness takes hold.

Liquid Pages of Reflection

A splash of ink on a rainy day,
Characters float in a watery ballet.
A pickle fights jelly in a vegetable war,
Worms read the news on the ocean floor.

Pondering life, a banana starts to muse,
Should I wear yellow or a festive red snooze?
In the sea of my thoughts, I paddle and twist,
Hoping for clarity but finding a twist.

Pages like rivers, they swirl and they spin,
Drowning in metaphors, where do we begin?
The fish tell me stories of wisdom afoul,
While a crab gives advice with a just puzzled scowl.

So let's drink in the words, let them roll around,
In puddles of laughter, we're happily drowned.
With every sip from this quirky aquarium,
We dive deeper still, oh, what a fun delirium!

The Breath of Hidden Narratives

In the attic lies a tome of delights,
Filled with unlikely tales of fruit fights.
Peaches wear glasses, and grapes play guitar,
In a world where a banana can drive a car.

Turn the page, hear the tomatoes debate,
Who's the best salad? It's really first-rate!
While onions just laugh, shedding layers of jest,
A book-loving carrot shouts, "I'm the best!"

Between lines of prose, giggles take flight,
As characters bicker all through the night.
With laughter that bubbles in every direction,
Who knew that stories could spark such affection?

So find your own voice in this wild symphony,
Dance with each metaphor, sing with glee.
In the breath of these tales, we all come alive,
And share in the chaos where silliness thrives.

Into the Depths of the Book

Dive into a tale where the absurd is ripe,
A goldfish becomes president after a hype.
With meetings held in a bubbling fishbowl,
And mermaids debating the merits of coal.

Each chapter's a sketch of the funniest sorts,
Where llamas wear tuxedos at start-up reports.
They pitch dreamy hats made of fluff and of fluff,
Claiming their inventions could never go rough.

From dragons who dance in the middle of roads,
To knights who tell jokes in their heavy, stiff loads.
In this circus of words, you'll roll on the floor,
As absurdity knocks on the literary door.

So pick up the book, let the nonsense ignite,
With every wild page, you're in for a fright.
In these depths, we chuckle 'til tears fill our eyes,
For in laughter's embrace, the true magic lies.

In the Shadows of Literature

In the library's dark, I seek my fate,
Among dusty tomes that can't quite wait.
They whisper secrets in muffled tones,
While I juggle pencils and dodge the drones.

A scruffy cat naps, judging my quest,
While I flip pages with fervor and zest.
Plot twists lurk like a mischievous game,
Should I laugh, cringe, or just feel the shame?

With coffee cups stacked like towers on high,
I swear these books have winked, oh my!
Characters dance on the edge of a line,
While my own plot twist continues to twine.

So here I sit, lost amid rhymes,
Wondering if I'm wasting my times.
Yet every page brings its own little cheer,
Who knows? Maybe my purpose is near!

The Quest for Hidden Truths

Through the pages, I awkwardly crawl,
Chasing truths that stand mighty and tall.
A plot that thickens like grandma's stew,
What's the moral? I haven't a clue!

There's a villain with shoes that squeak in rhyme,
And here I am, lost in my own mime.
Each chapter a riddle, each twist a whim,
Do I uncover wisdom or just get slim?

An old map crumpled, it leads me astray,
"Turn left at the dragons," it seems to say.
With side notes scribbled in ink that won't dry,
I stumble on jokes that make me just cry.

Yet, laughter bubbles, and at last, it's clear,
The truths I sought were always quite near.
Among grand adventures and heroes so bold,
The hidden is funny, like tales yet untold!

Pages that Speak

Oh, the pages converse in hushed tones,
Like gossipy friends mixing truth with puns.
"Have you met the knight with the tuba of gold?
His cat dinosaurs? Now that's a good fold!"

Each chapter's a party, from start to end,
Where the butler's a dragon and the soup's a trend.
Puns flip and swirl like a dance on a stage,
I laugh at my fate, this whimsical page.

Between lines of wisdom, wisdom turns sly,
These volumes, they giggle; oh my, oh my!
If plot devices had moods, I'd be a clown,
Tumbling through stories, wearing a crown.

So let's toast with tea made of poetic delight,
To the pages that speak, whether day or night.
With every word, I'm finding my knack,
In this bookish bazaar, there's no holding back!

A Symphony of Written Sorrows

In the quiet of prose, a wailing refrain,
Where characters sob over spilled coffee stains.
A tragic romance lost in a cringe,
Oh, how I giggle at every strange binge!

The author must've had a party gone wrong,
With villains in tutus singing sad songs.
I brace for the tears but burst into glee,
At the irony, misplaced, so uniquely free.

Every sonnet a symphony, sweetly absurd,
With metaphors tangled like some old bird.
Trying to weep on the very last page,
But laughing bursts through, inviting the sage.

So here's to the sorrows that tickle my bones,
For every sad tale, I've grinned 'til I moaned.
Between laughter and sighs, I scribble anew,
In this symphony of words, I'm laughing with you!

The Pages that Shape Us

In a world quite absurd, where odd tales spin,
I stumbled on a book, thought I'd take a win.
It promised me wisdom, but gave me a laugh,
A recipe for soup, that seemed to be half.

I flipped through the chapters, each hold a new jest,
Characters misfit, wearing moth-eaten vests.
I learned that if penguins can dance with great cheer,
Then surely my purpose is perfectly near.

A self-help guide said, 'Be the best you can!'
But told me to wear my socks like a fan.
A book on Zen spoke of inner delight,
But left me confused—now I'm stuck in a plight!

So here's to the pages that twist and that turn,
Through laughter and folly, there's much we can learn.
Perhaps it's in chaos our meaning resides,
Where humor sparks joy, and serendipity guides.

The Call of the Written Realm

In a land made of letters, where quills take flight,
A dragon once wrote me a poem at night.
It rhymed about snacks and a quest for good cheese,
I giggled so hard, I fell off my knees!

With a wink, an elf told me tales of old lore,
Of wizards, of goblins, that love to explore.
Instead of great battles, they held a cake race,
A farce, but I found my odd place in this space.

The parrot, quite wise, had a diploma in jokes,
He taught me the secrets of dragon-shaped cloaks.
With every mad creature, a charm to unveil,
I found my direction in whimsy-laden trails.

So heed the strange call from pages anew,
Where laughter is plenty and mischief is due.
The written realm beckons, so let's not be grim,
In a world full of fun, let's all take a swim!

The Journey of Ink and Intention

With a magnifying glass, I sought clear intent,
Inking my thoughts, from a cat in a tent.
The puns were relentless, the humor out loud,
As I searched for my path through the giggling crowd.

The map led to margins, where doodles take reign,
With comments from critics who only complain.
A pirate named Scribble led me to a feast,
Of cookies, and punch, with stories unleashed.

The ink spilled its secrets 'neath confetti and fun,
Each line held a riddle, with laughter hard-won.
And though my compass spun wildly with glee,
I found in this madness, the truest of me.

As the ink dried and settled, my heart felt so light,
In this boisterous journey, I squabbled and flight.
So I raise my quill high, with mischief I blend,
For in the adventure of words, I found a dear friend.

Soliloquies of the Soul

In the corner of quicksand, I penned down my woe,
With a chicken named Chuck, who could tango and flow.
He said, 'Don't be serious, it's all just a game!'
And sparked a rebellion, in a fort made of flame.

Each page sang a chorus of sillies and snipes,
As hedgehogs recited life's quirks with their pipes.
When pondering deep thoughts, they all kept it light,
With riddles and giggles that danced in the night.

The musings of squirrels, who juggled with zest,
Showed me that laughing was truly the best.
With echoes of chuckles wrapping round like a shawl,
The soliloquies crept in, inviting us all.

So I dip my quill in the joy that they spread,
For deep down inside, we all love to tread.
Through pages of nonsense, together we roam,
In a funny old world, we can always call home.

The Labyrinth of Literary Pursuits

In the library, I lost my way,
Books piled high, ready to play.
Turned left, turned right, where's that shelf?
Thought I'd find wisdom, found a dwarf elf.

A novel's plot twists like spaghetti,
Characters dance, aren't they petty?
Pages flipping at an alarming rate,
I just came for fun, not a blind date!

Every chapter's a wild rollercoaster,
Plot holes wider than an ocean's poster.
Laughter echoes through ink-stained halls,
Chasing phrases like silly balls.

With every story, I'll take a seat,
Shuffling through words can't be beat.
In this maze of whimsical tales,
I'll become a knight, sans armor, with pails.

Hidden Gems of Inspiration

In the attic, dust bunnies unite,
Old tomes sparkle, oh, what a sight!
Beneath the chaos, a gem I find,
A cookbook filled with poems, quite unlined.

Words strut around, in fancy shoes,
Some inspire, while others snooze.
A haiku about tacos? What a thrill!
The muse is a prankster, giving me chills.

Riddles and rhymes lie in wait,
Giggles abound as I contemplate.
I chuckle at nonsense, marvel at wit,
Words open doors, if only a bit.

So, gather the gems, polish each line,
Inspiration flows like a fine wine.
From pages so dusty, bright ideas bloom,
Laughter, my friend, is the best perfume!

Half-Thoughts and Full Hearts

My mind, a circus, thoughts juggle around,
Half-formed ideas scattered on the ground.
One whispers softly, another shouts loud,
Wandering through whims like a playful cloud.

Heart feels heavy, like a boulder at sea,
But laughter bubbles up, so wild and free.
In this jumble of moments, chaos is king,
Dancing on half-thoughts, oh, what a fling!

A puzzle of words forms a quirky face,
Dreams intertwined in a hasty embrace.
With every giggle, a truth comes to light,
Full hearts are filled in the midst of the night.

So here we are, in this playful bazaar,
Half-formed ideas, but we've come so far!
Let laughter lead, in every endeavor,
Our words may be silly, but joy lasts forever!

The Silence Between Sentences

Between two lines of text, a pause so grand,
Where whimsy dances, just as we planned.
In the silence, quirks come out to play,
   Even the punctuation wants to sway!

Words can chatter, but silence can sing,
An ellipsis giggles, 'Look what I bring!'
Laughing at commas that trip all around,
   Finding delight in each quirky sound.

The blank spaces whisper ridiculous dreams,
   Tickling thoughts with playful schemes.
Each sentence a feast, laughter's the spice,
   In between the words, everything's nice.

So embrace the silence, let it inspire,
For cozy moments sing louder than fire.
Between the lines, life can be strange,
But humor's the thread that happily chains.

Journeys in Unbound Text

In a library I stumbled, quite the sight,
With books stacked high, a dizzying height.
I reached for one, but it gave a shout,
"Not me today, you're in the wrong bout!"

Pages flapped like birds, taking flight,
A cookbook sneezed, what a bizarre fright!
Spaghetti swirled, oh what a dance,
Mistook it for steak, God, how it pranced!

A mystery novel whispered my name,
Told tales of crime, but with a scheme lame.
I tried to be clever, crack a case,
But tripped on a plot twist, my new face!

In this haven of chaos, I wear a grin,
Each tome a joke, let the laughter begin.
Life's quirks unravel, in words we play,
Who knew wisdom could tickle this way?

Navigating Literary Labyrinths

In the maze of pages, I lost my sense,
A romance took charge, all too intense.
With words like honey, sticky and sweet,
I fell for a character, quite the treat!

The shelves were tall, made me feel small,
An epic saga that was overdue a call.
I searched for answers, lost in the fray,
Found a plot twist instead, well, here we stay!

A guidebook chimed in, "Turn left at despair,"
So I laughed, thought, why go anywhere?
Did the map include snacks or a cozy chair?
Not all journeys matter, just make sure you're there!

But amidst the confusion, a chuckle rang true,
The stories we chase often chase us too.
In this wacky adventure, I found my quirks,
Navigating a labyrinth, where humor works!

Dreams Scripted in Stanzas

In stanzas I stumbled, a rhythmic spree,
Words bouncing around in a quirky jubilee.
A poet beckoned, his hat tipped just right,
"Join me, dear dreamer, let's dance through the night!"

Verses bubbled up like a soda pop can,
I swirled in the chaos, did the best I can.
With metaphors flying, like confetti in air,
Alliteration tickled, I couldn't help but share!

Similes grinned with a wink and a nudge,
"I'm more fun than a villain who won't budge!"
We penned a tale of whimsy and glee,
Where llamas recited poetry under a tree!

Each stanza a memory, a laugh to behold,
In dreams stitched together, stories unfold.
With nonsense and giggles, a playful delight,
In this scribbled world, everything felt right!

The Hidden Narrative

Between the lines, a riddle awaits,
A plot twist disguised among all the fates.
Characters hiding, plotting mischief galore,
Each word an adventure, opening a door!

In a tome of surprises, the ink spills across,
Characters complain, "The hero's a doss!"
While footnotes chuckle, making comments so sly,
Narrative whispers, "Don't you dare be shy!"

A protagonist fumbled, lost in a bind,
"Who's writing this chaos? I'm out of my mind!"
But with every mishap, a punchline arrives,
Where laughs mix with journeys, that's how it survives!

So here's to the stories that keep us bemused,
With comical charm, we're happily fused.
Embrace the absurd, let the narratives flow,
In the margins of laughter, the best tales will grow!

The Fabric of Storytelling

In a world of paper and glue,
Characters dance with a view.
Plots twist like spaghetti strands,
As ideas fly from writers' hands.

Pens leak secrets, oh what a sight!
Tales weave together, day and night.
Chasing laughter, dodging the tears,
Books play matchmaker for our fears.

Each chapter's a patch on life's quilt,
Stitching moments, love or guilt.
The heroes trip, the villains prance,
In every page, there's room to dance.

So grab a tale, let your mind soar,
Adventure awaits in every score.
With each turn, you'll giggle and sigh,
In the fabric of stories, you'll fly high.

A Canvas of Words

Words splash around like paint on a wall,
Creating pictures, both big and small.
A brush of humor, a stroke of wit,
On this canvas, every word's a hit!

Characters mingle, make silly faces,
Jumping through time and fun-filled places.
With dialogue that tickles your ears,
You'll find yourself wrapped up in cheers.

Plot twists somersault, flip, and dive,
Making sure your laughter survives.
As you read, you might just spill,
Your drink from laughter - what a thrill!

Every story painted, each line like a hue,
Brings joy and giggles, just for you.
So grab your brush, let's create a scene,
In the gallery of words, keep it keen!

The Archivist of Ambition

In a dusty library, dreams collect,
A jovial archivist takes a peek and then checks.
With a wink, they file stories galore,
Some tales are rich, while others are a bore!

They dance with volumes, a jolly great spree,
Cataloguing giggles and a bit of glee.
Each book that whispers, 'Open me wide,'
Prompts a chuckle that can't be denied.

With mismatched socks and a quirky hat,
This archivist knows where the fun is at.
Sorting ambition, but with flair so grand,
They'll make you laugh with a wave of their hand.

So if you're stuck in mundane routines,
Visit the archivist for some silly scenes.
From tales of heroes to cats that can sing,
In their treasure trove, joy's the true king!

Inked Dreams Awaiting

Behind every cover, dreams come alive,
Inked with giggles, where wishes thrive.
Chasing tales with mischievous glee,
A wild adventure, come ride with me!

Every page turn is a leap through time,
Witty punchlines and reasons to rhyme.
With quirky plots that twist and twirl,
In this world of ink, watch laughter unfurl.

Hidden in scripts, there's treasure untold,
Secrets of humor, pure and bold.
Dare to dive into stories that gleam,
Inked dreams awaiting, a reader's sweet dream!

So grab a pen, or just turn the page,
In this vast library, laughter's the stage.
With tales flowing free, there's always a chance,
To find joy in every whimsical dance.

Reflections in the Book of Life

In the silence of the shelf,
A cat reads with great stealth.
The author left a coffee stain,
Now it's nothing but a brain drain.

Chapters turn with a wink,
Narrator's voice starts to stink.
Characters run, oh what a sight,
Plot twists are rarely polite.

Bookmarks play hide and seek,
Often lost, but they don't speak.
Witty lines can make you grin,
While the climax decides to spin.

So laugh aloud in margin scrawls,
Life's too short for paper walls.
As you chase the pages' race,
Remember, it's a funny place!

The Marginalized Journey

In margins wide, sketch a face,
Lost in words, what a chase!
Every note a giggling spree,
A doodle ringed with irony.

Notes from distant lands drift in,
Drawn by thoughts, a little spin.
Swap your worries for a laugh,
As life drafts its own epitaph.

Between the lines, a squirrel talks,
Riding bicycles, sharing flocks.
Every footnote, a secret clue,
In this book, life's a comic brew.

Adventure waits on every page,
Turning chapters like a sage.
So, grab a pen, give it a whirl,
And let your laughter unfurl!

The Poetic Compass

With a compass lost, I roam,
Through stanzas, I've made my home.
Verses flirt, and rhymes collide,
A chance for fun on this wild ride.

In every word, a treasure hides,
Life's a joke that often bides.
On this path, I trip and fall,
While the meter has a ball.

Pages flip like summer dreams,
Where coffee spills are just routines.
Each pun dropped, a tickled pearl,
In the laughter, I twirl and swirl.

So laugh it off, embrace the detour,
With every line, the spirits soar.
In this compass made of ink,
Who needs a map? Just grab a drink!

Labyrinths of the Imagination

In a maze of thoughts I tread,
Wandering where wise men dread.
Turning pages, lost and found,
Each absurd plot twist astounds.

Characters trip on their own feet,
They tango with the plot's heartbeat.
Scribbled notes laugh in delight,
As they dance through day and night.

Ink spills hold a secret jest,
In labyrinths, you'll find the best.
Chasing tales, with every swoop,
Join the giggling literary troop.

So cherish words where humor reigns,
Life's just funny with a few trains.
In this maze, don't lose your flair,
Because laughter's the best affair!

Unwritten Destinies

In the library, I found a chair,
With dust bunnies swirling, I had a stare.
The books all giggled, they laughed with glee,
'What's your destiny, dear? It's all in the tea!'

I flipped through pages with wild delight,
Each turn a new tale, oh what a sight!
A knight and a dragon munching on fries,
Oh, these unwritten destinies wear silly disguises.

There's a goat with a cloak and a crown on his head,
Sipping hot cocoa, avoiding the dread.
"Just try the adventures," a book shouted loud,
"Life's a wild party, let's gather a crowd!"

So I danced between chapters, with laughter and cheer,
In a world full of whimsy, where nothing is clear.
With each turn of the page, a chuckle, a grin,
Finding my purpose in the nonsense within!

The Whispering Ink

In a quaint little shop, I found a small pen,
It whispered to me, 'Pick me up, come again!'
With ink that giggled and danced on the page,
It wrote me a letter, I must engage.

It scribbled my dreams in a frolicsome swirl,
'You're destined for laughter and a wiggly twirl!'
I peeked over shoulders of wise old tomes,
They hummed and they crooned, like old-fashioned gnomes.

Each line was a riddle, a joke to behold,
On a quest for the pleasure, not just the gold.
A chicken learned dancing, a turtle drove fast,
The charm of the stories, too good to last!

With pages that flutter, and ink that can sing,
I found my own purpose in everything!
In bursts of delight and carefree spins,
The whispers of ink wrote tales of my wins!

Scrolls of Unseen Horizons

I unrolled a scroll with a mischievous grin,
It spoke of adventures that would surely begin.
A pirate, a parrot, both giggling like fools,
Searching for treasure beneath jellybean pools.

The scroll twisted tales and tangled my fate,
As the characters plotted to open a gate.
A wizard who couldn't quite find his own hat,
"Is this magic or folly?" I pondered and sat.

With monsters who bake and cupcakes that roar,
Each scroll held a mystery, each turn opened more.
The ocean of stories, so wavy and bright,
I swam through the laughter, what a silly delight!

So many horizons, unseen yet so fun,
These scrolls bounced with joy, like a race just begun.
In the land of the whimsical, I twirled like a breeze,
Finding my essence with each laugh and tease!

Chapters of the Heart

In a bookshop of dreams, I opened my chest,
To discover the chapters I'd already guessed.
With characters silly, and plot twists to boot,
I laughed till I cried, what a glorious hoot!

Each page turned gently, like a tickling breeze,
A dragon who sneezed, scattering keys.
The words danced around, like a jester on stilts,
My heart was a canvas, awash with bright wits.

In tales that were hidden, or often ignored,
The fun and the laughter were always restored.
From heroes who tripped on their shoelaces tight,
To villains who can't seem to get things just right.

So each chapter I penned, infused with delight,
Was a whimsical journey, a piñata of light.
In the wildest of stories, I learned to believe,
That the heart finds its rhythm, in laughter we weave!

The Odyssey of the Written Word

Once I met a book, so wise and sage,
It said, "Dear reader, turn the page!"
I flipped and found a dancing cat,
Wearing a tie and talking like that.

The plot thickened like grandma's stew,
With knights who played the kazoo.
I laughed so hard, I spilled my tea,
A kingdom ruled by silliness, you see.

In every chapter, mischief did spread,
Like a rumor about the cat in my bed.
Each twist and turn left me grinning bright,
Where every dark knight turns into light.

So here's to the tales that bring us glee,
To questing knights and giggles, you see.
The journey unfolds in every line,
A world where nonsense and joy entwine.

The Haven Within the Covers

In the nook of my chair, I found a retreat,
A warm blanket and snacks, oh, what a treat!
Pages whisper secrets, oh so sly,
Of pirates and pizza, both sailing the sky.

Chapter one kicked off with a hilarious scene,
A robot who danced like it's on caffeine.
With every turn, my sides began to ache,
A dragon who juggles, for laughter's sake.

Pillow forts made from novels stacked high,
Where wise old owls wear a bowtie.
Each citation turned into a joke,
The plot thickens, yet hearts gently poke.

So let's read on, with a smile so wide,
Adventures await, with humor as guide.
In the covers, a haven we shall create,
Where laughter is king, and boredom's too late.

Ink-Soaked Revelations

On a rainy day, ink spilled on the floor,
An author got stuck in a fantastical lore.
With plot twists swirling, she couldn't get free,
A fish in a hat, what a sight to see!

She typed and she laughed, as the words ran wild,
A gerbil in glasses, oh look at that child!
Each revelation a quirky new gem,
Like pirates who dance in a glorious phlegm.

At coffee shops, they sip lattes so bold,
While dragons swap gossip, mouths open and cold.
Ink-soaked adventures, every line a delight,
With every odd creature, oh what a sight!

So here's to the whimsy that stories can weave,
With ink-stained fingers and hearts up the sleeve.
For every revelation, a chuckle draws near,
In this world of pages, we've nothing to fear.

The Language of the Inkwell

In the world of inkwells, where stories are born,
Words throw jellybeans, their laughs to adorn.
A gnome starts to croon with a voice like a bell,
While frogs join the fray with a musical swell.

Each stanza erupts like a popcorn surprise,
With pirouetting words dressed in piggy disguise.
The verbs wear pajamas, the nouns come to play,
In this quirky bazaar where nonsense holds sway.

Syntax and semantics threw a big bash,
With metaphors mosh-pitting, a colorful splash.
Adjectives jiggle, adverbs chimed in,
As the letters all twirled, wearing big grins.

So let's dive headfirst into this speckled delight,
Where the language of inkwells paints laughable sights.
With each quirky tale that we share in the night,
We swirl in the chaos, ready for flight.

Restless Words of Search

In a bookshop maze, I roam with glee,
Each title beckons, 'Come read me!'
Amid the shelves, I start to prance,
Chasing tales like a wild romance.

The novels whisper, 'Pick me, pick me!'
But oh, the cost is quite the fee!
With every turn, a twist awaits,
As I debate, should I tempt fate?

Humor hides in footnotes small,
While characters play catch, and I just fall.
I trip on plot holes, stumble on cues,
While my coffee goes cold, I've finished the blues.

Yet among the spines, I search and seek,
For laughter's joy makes my heart peak.
A treasure trove of wit I find,
In this wild love of words, I'm intertwined.

The Garden of Literary Wonders

In the garden where pages bloom,
Imagination spills from every room.
Characters dance like bees in flight,
Crafting stories from morning to night.

Plot twists grow like odd-shaped trees,
While metaphors sway in the gentle breeze.
I prune my thoughts with a giggle and snort,
As I tend to tales of whimsy and sport.

Ink-stained petals in colors bright,
Invite me to laugh till the morning light.
Each story sprout offers a favor,
To tickle my mind is the greatest labor.

So here I dig, with a trowel of wit,
In this garden of words, I happily sit.
With each new chapter, I giggle and snort,
In this rich soil of prose, I'm truly caught.

Shadows Among the Stanzas

In the quiet corners, shadows play,
With every word, they dance away.
Rhymes giggle, their secrets unfurl,
Creating mischief in a literary whirl.

Every stanza is a cheeky grin,
And the plots thicken with a whimsical spin.
Characters sneak in with a friendly wave,
As they plot out how to misbehave.

Pages rustle with playful pranks,
While I laugh at wordy hijinks and janks.
Footnotes poke fun at the wise and the bold,
In this shadowy world, stories unfold.

So I wander, lost in their spree,
In a verse-riddled realm where I am free.
With each line I read, I chuckle aloud,
In the shadows of stanzas, I'm delightfully proud.

The Path of Quill and Reflection

With a quill in hand, I meander the line,
Writing nonsense, believing I'm divine.
Reflections of thoughts that tiptoe and hop,
In a jumbled ballet, I can't seem to stop.

Every word spills like tea from a cup,
As I ponder if it's time to give up.
But oh! The joy when they start to rhyme,
It's like I've won the wordy lottery, prime time!

I dance with metaphors, trade jests with verbs,
While imaginary friends shout their curbside flurbs.
Eureka! A punchline - I've struck writing gold,
In this path of quill, laughter never gets old.

So here's to the scribbles and giggles that flow,
Through reflections of nonsense where good humor grows.
In each little line, I find my delight,
On this whimsical journey, everything feels right.

www.ingramcontent.com/pod-product-compliance
Lightning Source LLC
Chambersburg PA
CBHW051636160426
43209CB00004B/669